THE ROMEO INITIATIVE

Also by Trina Davies:
Shatter

THE
ROMEO
INITIATIVE

TRINA DAVIES

**PLAYWRIGHTS
CANADA PRESS**
TORONTO

PLAYWRIGHTS CANADA PRESS
The Canadian Drama Publisher
215 Spadina Ave., Suite 230, Toronto, ON, Canada M5T 2C7
phone 416.703.0013 fax 416.408.3402
info@playwrightscanada.com • www.playwrightscanada.com

For professional or amateur production rights, please contact:
Michael Petrasek at Kensington Literary Representation
34 St. Andrew Street, Toronto, ON M5T 1K6
416.979.0187, kensingtonlit@rogers.com

Playwrights Canada Press acknowledges the financial support of the Government of Canada through the Canada Book Fund and the Canada Council for the Arts, and of the Province of Ontario through the Ontario Arts Council and the Ontario Media Development Corporation, for our publishing activities.

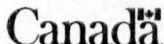 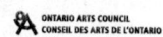 

Cover art and design by Patrick Gray
Book design by Blake Sproule

LIBRARY AND ARCHIVES CANADA CATALOGUING IN PUBLICATION
Davies, Trina
      The Romeo initiative / Trina Davies.

A play.
Issued also in electronic format.
ISBN 978-1-77091-053-9

      I. Title.

PS8607.A9526R76 2012   C812'.6   C2012-901264-5

First edition: May 2012
Printed and bound in Canada by Marquis Imprimeur, Montreal

For my girls. Taunya, Glenda, Pam, Shannon, Jau-ruey, Elena, Mari, Jennifer, Lyrissa.

The Romeo Initiative premiered as part of the twenty-fifth edition of the Enbridge playRites Festival of New Canadian Plays on February 2, 2011, at Alberta Theatre Projects, Calgary. It featured the following cast and creative team:

Karin Maynard: Kira Bradley
Markus Richter: Christian Goutsis
Lena Hahn: Jamie Konchak

Director: Glenda Stirling
Set designer: Scott Reid
Costume designer: Jenifer Darbellay
Lighting designer: David Fraser
Sound designer/composer: Kevin McGugan
Dramaturg: Amy Lynn Strilchuk
Stage manager: Marcie Januska
Assistant stage manager: Tuled Giovanazzi

NOTES

No accents are to be used in this play.

Each act has its own distinctive emotion and feel. This should be evident through lighting and sound that are decidedly different in each act.

Within each act, no blackouts should occur.

Where slashes (/) appear, the lines of dialogue overlap, but the audience should hear every word.

If an intermission is desired, the playwright suggests it should occur between acts one and two.

The laws of love, I assume, like the laws of gravity, apply everywhere.

—Anna Funder, *Stasiland*

How small, of all that human hearts endure
That part which laws or Kings can cure.

—Samuel Johnson

The spy agency did not follow the rules and regulations of either a girls' school or the Salvation Army.

—Markus Wolf, head of East German Stasi, when questioned about the Romeo initiative

CHARACTERS

Karin (KAH rin) Maynard—in her thirties
Markus Richter—late thirties to early forties
Lena Hahn—mid to late twenties

ACT I
A LOVE STORY

*Act I is heightened, dreamy, in look and feel.
This should be reflected in staging and the
soundscape, which should be soft, magical, epic.*

1. Black Sea Coast

The sound of waves crashing onto a beach. Soothing.

A woman, KARIN, in her thirties, dressed smartly, sits at a bistro table near the Black Sea. She is reading a book, looking up occasionally to admire the sun setting over the waves. There is coffee in a fine cup in front of her.

The sound of the waves increases. She pauses, puts down her book, and sips her coffee, then picks up the book again and continues reading.

A good-looking man in a good-quality suit, in his late thirties or early forties, enters tentatively. He walks across the stage, looking for someone. There is no one. He crosses the length of the stage, looks offstage, at a loss, and wanders back again. He stands uncertainly. The woman notices.

The man sees the woman watching him and acknowledges her, embarrassed to have attracted attention. He continues to stand and twitch. Very long pause.

The man looks for a place to sit. There is only the extra chair at the bistro table. The woman sees him regard the chair. They both look at the chair intently. Finally she looks at him and shrugs. He takes the chair nervously and sits. Pause.

MARKUS   Thank you.

KARIN   Pardon?

MARKUS   Thank you. For the chair. *(beat)* For letting me sit.

KARIN   Oh.

MARKUS   It was very kind.

KARIN   It was nothing.

MARKUS   There was nowhere else to sit.

Pause. She tries to read her book. He looks out at the waves.

Restorative.

KARIN   What?

MARKUS   Restorative. The waves. That's what the brochure said. "Be restored."

KARIN   Yes?

MARKUS   That's what it said. I had hopes.

KARIN   Of being restored?

MARKUS   Yes. You?

KARIN   It's only a vacation.

MARKUS   Oh. Where did you find the coffee?

KARIN   The man brought it.

> *MARKUS looks around in vain for "the man."*

MARKUS   That book…

KARIN   Yes?

MARKUS   Where did you find that book?

KARIN   *(looking at the book, shrugging)* A bookstore in Bonn. Why?

MARKUS   Bonn? Really.

KARIN   Yes. Why do you ask?

MARKUS   Do you like it?

KARIN   I suppose. I haven't read very much of it yet.

MARKUS   It's an unusual topic. For a woman.

KARIN   Pardon?

MARKUS   I didn't mean… I mean you must have a fine mind. That's what I meant.

KARIN   *(unsure)* Thank you.

MARKUS   You're from Bonn?

KARIN   No… I… yes, I suppose I'm from Bonn.

MARKUS   Not originally, then?

KARIN   No. Originally from Stuttgart.

MARKUS   My mother is from Stuttgart! She was an opera singer. Have you been to the Stuttgart opera?

KARIN   *(interested)* Why yes, I have. Your mother sang there?

MARKUS   Yes. I'm told she was quite good. A diva even.

KARIN   She no longer sings?

MARKUS   No.

KARIN   Why?

MARKUS   Love. She married a storekeeper. My father saw her perform one night and was relentless. Pursued her night and day.

One dozen roses each performance. He would stand at the stage door every night. Just for a glimpse. Never speaking.

He catches her gaze, a beat, they look away.

KARIN   And then?

MARKUS   And then?

KARIN   She knew it was him, and then what?

MARKUS   Well… that's all she said about it really.

KARIN   There must be more to the story.

MARKUS   I suppose. I never asked.

KARIN   She married him?

MARKUS   Oh yes. She would sing around the house sometimes. To her little babies. To me, as a child.

KARIN   What would she sing?

MARKUS   Oh, *Romeo and Juliet*, or *Tristan and Isolde*. She was a romantic.

KARIN   She had to be.

MARKUS   Why is that?

KARIN   To marry the silent man with the roses.

MARKUS   Yes, I suppose.

          Pause.

KARIN   It is a bit restorative, I think.

MARKUS   The waves?

KARIN   Yes. There's something about water.

MARKUS   Yes. I think there is.

          She drinks.

KARIN   I shouldn't drink my coffee when you haven't any. Perhaps
            I can find the man for you…

MARKUS   Oh, don't bother. It's fine. I should probably be getting back.

KARIN   You're here alone?

MARKUS   Yes… that is…

KARIN   I shouldn't have pried.

MARKUS   No… no, it's fine. Are you… here… alone?

KARIN   I… needed a vacation.

MARKUS   I see.

KARIN   By myself, yes.

MARKUS   Away from your/

KARIN   Oh no/

MARKUS   husband/

KARIN   I haven't got any/

MARKUS   I'm/

KARIN   What of your/

MARKUS   I shouldn't have/

KARIN   wife/

MARKUS   I haven't got a/

KARIN   I haven't got/

MARKUS/KARIN   Anyone.

> *They look awkwardly around the space. Pause.*

MARKUS   I think I see the… the man… I'll just go and ask him for
           some… if it's all right… if you don't mind…

KARIN   No, no of course…

Markus rises from the table and moves offstage to order and collect his coffee. Karin rummages through her handbag, looking for something furiously. She finds her compact, pulls it out, and tries to check and fix her face and hair as quickly as possible. While she is doing this, Markus returns. She awkwardly stashes the compact.

Oh, here it is... I was... looking for this... for my... *(She pulls out what she grabs first.)* room key.

MARKUS   *(beat)* Room key.

KARIN   *(realizing)* No! I...! *(beat)* I was afraid I'd lost it... for a moment.

MARKUS   Oh. Well, that's good luck then.

             Markus drinks.

             It's awful.

KARIN   Yes.

MARKUS   You should have warned me.

KARIN   I thought you might have expected. Bulgaria and all.

MARKUS   Yes. It's almost as bad as the East German swill.

KARIN   You're German.

MARKUS   Naturally. Although I work everywhere.

KARIN   You've been to East Berlin?

MARKUS   Yes. Grey people, grey buildings… mostly, well…

KARIN   Dull. I've heard that.

MARKUS   Yes, dull.

KARIN   Your work took you there? What do you do?

MARKUS   I was there briefly once. I do aid work, mostly.

KARIN   That must be fulfilling.

MARKUS   It is. But it's… difficult… sometimes. So many people. So many people, and you simply can't help them all. Sometimes a person feels a bit… useless.

KARIN   Each person must do what an individual can. To change the world.

MARKUS   That's a marvellous way to look at it.

KARIN   I'm sure you're doing what one person can. Probably much more than most.

MARKUS   Yes. If you look at it that way…

KARIN   I think it's quite noble.

MARKUS   Do you?

KARIN   Sacrificing for what one believes in. It takes character. *(beat, considering him)* I think you have character.

MARKUS   Thank you. I do feel it's important to sacrifice for what one believes in.

KARIN   I can tell that about you.

MARKUS   You can?

KARIN   Something in the eyes…

> *They lock eyes for a moment too long. Both reach for their coffee.*

MARKUS   It's starting to get dark.

KARIN   Yes.

MARKUS   I suppose that's that then.

KARIN   Pardon?

MARKUS   I was… supposed to… meet someone.

KARIN   *(disappointed)* Oh…

MARKUS   It appears I have been turned aside.

He shrugs a bit sadly, won't meet her eyes.

KARIN   Oh.

MARKUS   Too much to hope for, I suppose. Restoration. *(beat)* It's quite embarrassing, really. I don't know why I told you.

KARIN   Oh, please, don't be embarrassed...

MARKUS   I suppose I had hopes. Silly really. I blame my mother. And opera.

KARIN   You surely don't give up so easily. What of your father, and the roses...?

MARKUS   I actually expect I was saved from a pretty dull evening.

KARIN   But you had hopes.

MARKUS   Of meeting someone. Yes.

Pause. They look at each other.

The gulls cry. The sun sets.

4. *The Reception*

> *A desk appears in front of KARIN. She sits, attending to pa-perwork. There is an old-fashioned intercom system and a telephone on the desk. LENA, a good-looking woman in her twenties, is dressed in a sophisticated and sexy style. She has a scarf. LENA is fidgeting in a waiting chair. She stands up, looks at a piece of art, sits down again. She stands up again.*

LENA   This is ridiculous.

KARIN   I'm sure he'll be able to see you soon/

LENA   Call him again.

KARIN   Lena, he said that he'd/

LENA   I don't care what he said before.

KARIN   *(trying to finish her sentence)* that he'd come out as soon as/

LENA   He can't leave me out here, I have things to do.

KARIN   As soon as he's finished/

LENA   Karin—I'm bored!

> *Pause.*

KARIN   There are some magazines there... *(indicating)*

> *LENA curls her lip. She walks over to KARIN's desk.*

LENA   What's his wife like?

> *KARIN ignores her.*

Is she pretty? Is she old and wrinkly? Is she huge as a whale? *(pause)* He's not paying attention like he did before...

> *LENA appears visibly upset. KARIN watches her.*

KARIN   He seems to love you.

LENA   *(brightening)* Do you think so?

KARIN   Yes.

LENA   He wouldn't leave me?

KARIN   Well... I...

LENA   *(getting upset)* Oh...

KARIN   I'm sure he loves you.

LENA   How can you tell?

KARIN   Well... he has me send you flowers every week.

LENA   Flowers aren't love.

KARIN   And he talks about you all the time.

LENA   He does?

KARIN   And he brightens up and smiles when he knows he's going to see you.

LENA   Really?

KARIN   And he always takes your calls and lets you in right away. *(beat)* Oh.

LENA   I knew it!

KARIN   It's… it's just a very important call. He's talking to the American consulate.

LENA   That's what I love so about my Hermann. He is so dedicated, so committed to building a better West.

      Pause.

      So that makes you sure, does it? That he loves me. That he does those things.

KARIN   Yes, of course.

      Pause.

LENA   Do you have a boyfriend?

KARIN   No... I...

LENA   You hesitated.

KARIN   *(firmly)* No. I don't.

LENA   Why did you hesitate? You do, don't you. I know you
            do! Tell me! Imagine that—little miss serious, little miss
            mouse, lands a man in Bonn, the spinster wasteland of
            the Western world.

KARIN   Well I don't think/

LENA   It's true. Do you know how many more single women
            there are in Bonn than single men? It's atrocious! All of
            them moping about, sitting home on Friday night be-
            cause they can't be seen going out alone. Take it from me.
            I'm sitting in a waiting room, all dressed up, waiting for
            a married man to leave his telephone call and pay atten-
            tion to me. Come on, mouse. Spill it.

            *KARIN ignores LENA. LENA drums her fingers on a sur-
            face to get attention. This doesn't work. She starts to move
            objects around loudly, like a petulant child.*

KARIN   I have work to do.

LENA   You're supposed to entertain guests.

KARIN   I'm supposed to provide a comfortable place for people
          to wait.

LENA   All I asked for was the story. About the "non boyfriend."
          It's not asking for much. *(KARIN ignores her.)* Don't you
          trust me?

KARIN   No.

LENA   I'm hurt! *(beat)* You're cold. A cold fish, you know that?
          (She starts to chant.) Tell me tell me tell me tell me/

KARIN   You're acting like a child.

LENA   Better than an old maid.

KARIN   That's— *(She stops herself.)* If I tell you will you stop?

LENA   Yes! Yes of course.

KARIN   All right. I met him on holiday abroad and yesterday…
          yesterday I went to my favourite bookstore and he was
          there.

          Beat.

LENA   You're right. You don't have a boyfriend. *(a pause as
          she fidgets)* Why won't he come out of that room! I'm
          hungry!

          KARIN works. LENA thumbs through a magazine.

He didn't ask you for dinner?

KARIN   Who?

LENA   The invisible boyfriend.

KARIN   Oh. No. I told you it was/

LENA   Did you leave something behind?

KARIN   What?

LENA   *(sighs)* My god you're hopeless. You've got to leave a glass slipper behind. Some excuse, some reason he has to contact you.

KARIN   I don't believe in fairy tales.

LENA   But what if they believe in you?

KARIN   Then they'll be disappointed.

            The door to the outside opens and MARKUS enters. The women freeze. Pause.

MARKUS   Excuse me, I... Yes. Hello.

LENA   *(impressed)* Hello. You know, if you're here to see Hermann, you'll have to get in line.

MARKUS   Pardon?

LENA   I'm just saying I'm first, that's all. Unless you're going to do something that will change my mind.

MARKUS   Hello, Karin. You said yesterday about working at the Federal Ministry of Economics/

LENA   Oh! Is this… *(looking over to KARIN)*

KARIN   Yes. Are you here for Mr. Baum…?

MARKUS   What? No, I… I thought I'd come over to say hello.

KARIN   Oh.

LENA   *(mocking)* Oh.

An awkward pause. They all look at each other.

Well, for my part, I'm glad to have the company. Karin here isn't much of a conversationalist, Mr.…?

MARKUS   Richter.

LENA   Mr. Richter. Come and sit by me, we can wait together.

MARKUS   I don't think… I can't stay.

LENA   Oh, you can't go now! It would be cruel to show up and then leave me to the cold cold world all by myself.

MARKUS   I think you'll do just fine. Karin, I wondered if you might like to go for dinner tonight? That is, if you don't have plans.

LENA   Plans? Miss Mouse?

The phone rings, KARIN picks it up.

KARIN   Yes, sir, I'll let her know/

LENA grabs the phone from KARIN's hands.

LENA   Darling! I'm simply dying from waiting for you! You must
            come out this instant... this instant, or I'll... I'll never
            speak to you again, I'll... *(KARIN and MARKUS consider each
            other.)* I will! You'll never see me or my sweet— Really?
            Darling. You have to promise me, you have to promise, or
            I swear I'll... Yes.

She kisses into the phone and hangs it up.

*LENA stands and straightens her appearance. She smiles
devilishly.*

I'm going in. He says you're to take a long lunch. *(beat)*

*LENA looks at MARKUS and slips off her scarf effort-
lessly, leaving it on the couch while looking at KARIN.
She exits through the interior office door. The loud
sounds of a man and a woman laughing and carrying on come through the door. MARKUS and KARIN
are embarrassed.*

MARKUS   I hope you don't/

KARIN   I don't.

MARKUS   That's good, because I wouldn't want/

KARIN   It's fine.

> *KARIN turns and straightens her desk nervously, her back to MARKUS.*

MARKUS   I admire your... *(She turns around.)* Um, your dedication. And your choice in books. Dinner tonight, eight p.m.?

KARIN   I... actually I have a lot of work to catch up on tonight, and/

MARKUS   Then maybe lunch?

> *KARIN hesitates. A loud sound from behind the closed door.*

KARIN   Yes, please.

> *The scene shifts. MARKUS takes KARIN to a restaurant, where they sit.*

5. Lunch

> *MARKUS and KARIN are sitting at a restaurant. They have finished their meals and have coffee cups in front of them.*

MARKUS   Thanks for meeting me again.

KARIN   Thank you for lunch. Again.

MARKUS   You're welcome. More coffee?

KARIN   No, thank you. I should be getting back to the office.

MARKUS   Do I make you uncomfortable?

KARIN   What?

MARKUS   You're always running away.

KARIN   No, I don't mean to/

MARKUS   Always getting back to important work. I've really en-
            joyed the last three days. Seeing you. Being with you.

KARIN   I'm sorry if I seem ungrateful, it's just that it's/

MARKUS   A very busy time at work. I understand.

KARIN   I shouldn't go on about it, it's not like what I do is more
            important than what you do. In fact, I admire you. Wish
            I did what you do—it's so much more… direct.

            MARKUS reaches for and holds KARIN's hand. She is ner-
            vous, but allows it.

MARKUS   Karin, I/

KARIN   *(dodging)* You get to look into the eyes of the people you
            help/

MARKUS   I feel/

KARIN   That has to be satisfying.

       Beat.

MARKUS   *(pulling back)* It is.

       Beat.

KARIN   I wish I had that kind of… meaning… to what I do.

MARKUS   I'm addicted to it. I think it started when I was doing my first fieldwork, sleeping in a tent for one of the first times in my life. It was morning, still dark, and I heard this whispering. A young boy, maybe eight, asked me to come with him. He said his mother needed help. It was only after I was following him that it occurred to me that it wasn't a very good idea, that it could be a trap, a way to kidnap a foreign aid worker.

KARIN   But it wasn't.

MARKUS   No, it wasn't.

       LENA enters behind them in her outdoor coat, carrying a package. She listens, unnoticed.

Lucky for me. It could have been, stupid as I was then. But we didn't walk far before I saw the woman in the bushes. The boy's mother. The two of them had gone out in early morning to gather firewood. She was in labour. I panicked, told the boy that they needed someone else, someone trained, a doctor… but it was already too late. I knelt down and…

KARIN   Delivered a baby!

MARKUS   Yes.

He takes KARIN's hand in his.

LENA   Good to know that you have useful skills. Let me guess, they named the baby Markus?

KARIN   Did they?

MARKUS   As a matter of fact they did. They were so… grateful, so happy. I knew then that I'd found what I was supposed to do. Not delivering babies, obviously, but helping people. I'm funding the boy Markus's schooling/

LENA   So generous of you! Hello, Karin. So you did take my advice! I knew you'd love this place. The atmosphere is superb!

MARKUS   On your way somewhere?

LENA   Oh, just to mail this package. Hermann was getting quite upset, Karin, that you hadn't returned from lunch on time again, but not to worry. I covered for you, told him I'd take the package for mailing.

KARIN   I should get back. *(She starts to get up.)*

LENA starts to undo her coat, lays the package on the table. LENA takes KARIN's chair as KARIN stands up.

MARKUS   I'm sure you don't have to go just yet. Lena? I'm sure you've bought Karin a few minutes more?

MARKUS entreats KARIN to sit in his chair. He stands.

LENA   Hm? Yes, I'm sure you won't be missed.

KARIN   I'll take the package.

She reaches for it but LENA pulls it back.

LENA   No, no problem. I said I'd take it and I will. It's just some silly organizational charts or some such nonsense. Honestly, I don't see what the big deal is anyhow.

KARIN   He showed them to you?

LENA   Sure. He seems quite excited about it all, so I play along. "Yes, dear, that's very impressive, dear." Why? Are they confidential or something?

MARKUS   Coffee?

LENA   Yes, please. And I'm famished. Surely there's dessert or something around here. It's hard covering for you two.

MARKUS goes to retrieve the coffee and a menu.

KARIN   I never asked/

LENA   Consider it a good deed.

KARIN   I don't need you to cover for me.

LENA   No?

KARIN   No.

LENA   Fine. Next time he's roaring about where you are I'll tell
           him you're out for lunch with your invisible boyfriend.

KARIN   He's going away.

LENA   So there won't be anything to cover up then, will there.

KARIN   No.

LENA   You look… brighter. Did you get a new haircut?

KARIN   No. *(She touches her hair, blushes.)*

LENA   Ah.

KARIN   Ah?

LENA   *(smiling)* Never mind. I know.

           MARKUS returns with the coffee and menu.

KARIN   I need to get back to the office.

LENA   But I just got here.

           KARIN prepares to leave.

KARIN   Thank you for lunch. Again.

           *She exits hastily but MARKUS stops her a distance from
           the table. LENA watches them but can't hear what they're
           saying.*

MARKUS   Karin! Wait. I just wanted to ask you… can I write you
           while I'm away?

KARIN   Write me?

MARKUS   Would that be all right?

KARIN   Markus, I don't mean to act like…

MARKUS   I know. I'm going away.

KARIN   I have to get back to the office. *(She turns to go, turns back
           to him.)* I'd like it if you wrote to me.

MARKUS   You'll write back?

           *KARIN pauses, nods. MARKUS draws her in for a short,
           sweet kiss. Their first. KARIN leaves quickly.*

LENA   You'll join me in a crème caramel, will you? After all, I
        just arrived…

        *MARKUS reluctantly returns to the table and sits beside
        LENA.*

7. Karin's Letter

*KARIN is writing. In another space, MARKUS reads her
letter, smiles, and puts it someplace safe.*

KARIN   Markus, thank you so much for your letter. I think about you
        all the time. I'm waiting anxiously for the day you return.
        (She crumples the letter, starts again.) Dear Markus. Thanks
        for the letter. Things are going well here. Sincerely, Karin.

8. A Momentous Date

*MARKUS and KARIN have just entered KARIN's apart-
ment. They're wet, it's been raining. MARKUS carries a
dripping umbrella. They look at each other, unsure of
what to do next.*

KARIN   Oh! I should…

She gestures to take his coat.

MARKUS   *(finding a place for the umbrella and handing her his coat)*
           Yes. Thank you.

           MARKUS fidgets awkwardly by the door.

KARIN   Would you like to come in?

MARKUS   Thank you. I like your apartment. It's very… clean.

KARIN   Thank you.

           MARKUS stands in the middle of the room.

           Would you like to… sit?

           MARKUS sits. KARIN sits. A pause.

           A drink?

MARKUS   Yes. That would be nice.

           KARIN gets up to pour a highball.

           I've really loved tonight. It's been so good to see you.

KARIN   Me too. Loved tonight.

MARKUS   I've… thought about you.

KARIN   I've thought about you too.

MARKUS   You have?

KARIN   Yes.

MARKUS   I like that.

KARIN   I'm glad.

MARKUS   What have you thought about?

> *He touches her arm or her leg.*

KARIN   Uh... seeing you?

MARKUS   Yes? I've thought about other things too.

KARIN   *(nervously)* Yes?

MARKUS   Yes.

> *He is close to her now, moving in.*

KARIN   Like... like what things?

MARKUS   Like... this...

> *He pulls her to him and kisses her forcefully.*

KARIN　　Markus... I just don't know that we're... that I'm... ready...

MARKUS　　Oh?

A long pause. He backs off. He stands up and takes his glass back to the bar area.

Oh. That's fine. It's better this way.

KARIN　　What?

MARKUS　　It's probably for the best.

KARIN　　What do you mean?

MARKUS　　That we not get too involved.

KARIN　　What are you saying?

MARKUS　　That you're being smart. It's the right decision.

KARIN　　No, I/

MARKUS　　I'm away with work all the time/

KARIN　　No! Markus, I didn't mean.../

MARKUS　　I'm not a very good catch for a girl like you.

Beat. KARIN reaches out to comfort him.

KARIN   I'm sorry. I… I do want to kiss you, you know.

MARKUS   You do?

KARIN   I do.

She pulls him towards her, kisses him.

MARKUS   No. No, you were right, it isn't a good idea…

KARIN   No, I was wrong, I was just/

MARKUS   Maybe we shouldn't/

KARIN   No, no I want to/

MARKUS   My schedule is out of control/

KARIN   I just wasn't sure that you/

MARKUS   Work is very important, I can't just/

KARIN   would respect me, and/

MARKUS   be thinking about someone else when/

KARIN   I didn't want you to think I was easy/

MARKUS   I should be taking care of those that need/

KARIN   No girl wants to think that she's/

MARKUS   my help/

KARIN   easy, but I/

MARKUS   I shouldn't be acting like a teenager.

KARIN   really care for you.

MARKUS   If I could only... DAMMIT!

       KARIN approaches MARKUS. She kisses him.

KARIN   I don't want to talk anymore.

       Lights shift.

9. The Panties

       MARKUS and KARIN are in bed. KARIN is sleeping. MARKUS gets up without waking her. He starts to go through the clothing that has been strewn on the floor, looking for something. He watches KARIN, careful not to wake her. He finds what he's looking for. He collects his briefcase, brings it over, takes a pen, and slowly picks up KARIN's panties from the floor with the pen, balancing them, about to put them in his briefcase, when she wakes up.

KARIN   What are you doing?

MARKUS   *(startled)* What!?

KARIN   What are you doing.

MARKUS   *(He drops the objects.)* Nothing... I...

KARIN   Is that my underwear?

MARKUS   No, I was... tidying up... I was...

KARIN   What were you doing with my underwear?

MARKUS   Nothing! I told you, I was...

KARIN   Tidying up...

MARKUS   Yes.

KARIN   My underwear.

MARKUS   Yes.

KARIN   Just my underwear.

MARKUS   No, not exactly, I...

KARIN   By putting it into your briefcase.

MARKUS   I wasn't...

KARIN   You were! I saw you!

MARKUS   I… *(He sits down on the bed, defeated.)* All right. All right, yes.

KARIN   Why?

MARKUS   I… I'm embarrassed.

KARIN   Embarrassed about what?

MARKUS   It's been such a long time…

KARIN   What are you talking about?

MARKUS   It's been so long since I've seen you last and I… well… I…

KARIN   Markus?

MARKUS   Well… I guess I wanted to take a part of you with me. That's all. Now I'm embarrassed.

KARIN   *(She holds him.)* That's sweet!

MARKUS   *(more embarrassed)* I'm glad you think so.

KARIN   That is so…

MARKUS   Sweet?

KARIN   Yes! Well, and maybe a bit strange.

MARKUS   That's why… you were asleep!

KARIN   You wanted to take a part of me with you!

MARKUS   Yes, okay. Can we talk about something else.

KARIN   You like me.

MARKUS   Yes…

KARIN   You love me…

MARKUS   Yes…

KARIN   You want to carry my underwear…

MARKUS   Not "carry" it exactly, I'm not/

       KARIN kisses him. She looks at him expectantly.

    What?

KARIN   Well, aren't you going to put them in your briefcase?

MARKUS   What?

KARIN   Here.

       She hands them to him.

MARKUS   Uh… thanks.

       He puts the panties in his briefcase. Beat.

KARIN   That's kind of dirty, you know.

MARKUS   Here, have them back…

KARIN   No, no… Come here.

> *She wraps herself around him. She smells his hair, his neck. Pause.*

MARKUS   I have to tell you… something. *(beat)* You're… not going to like it.

> *KARIN releases him.*

KARIN   What?

MARKUS   There's… a complication.

> *KARIN gets quiet. Long pause.*

KARIN   You're married.

MARKUS   What? No!/

KARIN   Then what/

MARKUS   It's not a/

KARIN   I knew it couldn't/

MARKUS   What are you talking/

KARIN   be this easy, I knew/

MARKUS   Stop talking and listen to me!!

           KARIN stops. Regards him.

           I have to go away… for… longer than I told you.

KARIN   What? How long?

MARKUS   Six weeks. Maybe two months.

KARIN   Two months! You said a couple of weeks, you said/

MARKUS   I know what I said. I just couldn't. I couldn't bear the look
           on your face when I told you, and I wanted us to have a
           nice time while we were together. I thought/

KARIN   That you'd just disappear for two months?

MARKUS   No… maybe I could make it shorter, or I could tell you
           from there…

KARIN   So why tell me now?

MARKUS   I had to tell you. It's all I thought about last night. The
           political situation has become more… complicated. *(He
           sighs.)* More complicated than it should be…

KARIN   What is it?

MARKUS   It's nothing. *(beat)* I'll miss you. I'll miss you every day.

KARIN   You'll have my underwear.

MARKUS   That's not funny. You don't realize what you mean to me.

KARIN   So much that you have to run away for two months.

MARKUS   You know I don't want to. You know that.

KARIN   *(grudgingly)* I know…

MARKUS   I have a present for you.

KARIN   Present?

MARKUS   I wanted to give you something… to think of me…

> *He presents a gift in a bag, which he had hidden in the room. She takes it.*

KARIN   A present! Really?

MARKUS   Really.

> *She opens it. It is an older style, out-of-fashion handbag.*

KARIN   It's… a handbag?

MARKUS   You like it?

KARIN   Yes… I…

MARKUS   You don't like it.

KARIN   No! I…

MARKUS   I thought about jewellery, but then I thought that's so ordinary, and I wanted something that you would carry with you every day. You don't like it.

KARIN   No, of course… it's very thoughtful.

MARKUS   Look inside.

KARIN   Yes, it's very nice.

MARKUS   In the inside pocket.

                    She pulls out a small glass vial full of sand.

KARIN   Sand?

MARKUS   Sand. So you'll remember.

KARIN   Did you take this from the beach where we met?

MARKUS   *(dodging, sheepish)* You can carry it all the time.

KARIN   Yes.

MARKUS   I guess it wasn't a very good idea. I just thought…

KARIN   It's a fantastic idea!

MARKUS   *(brightening)* It is?

KARIN   Yes, thank you.

MARKUS   *(noticing the time)* I'm going to be late.

             MARKUS gets up to leave

KARIN   Wait! I have something for you…

             She presses a small gift (unseen) into his hand from hers.

             Don't open it here. Wait.

MARKUS   Thank you. I have to go. Don't forget me.

KARIN   Never.

             He exits. Alone, she smoothes out the blankets on the bed.

             The scene shifts, KARIN takes the handbag to her desk.

14. Jealous

The ministry. KARIN is alone. She rifles through papers on her desk, looking for something. LENA enters and quietly watches. KARIN puts a manila envelope in her handbag.

LENA   What are you doing?

KARIN   *(jumping)* What?

LENA   What are you doing there?

KARIN   Nothing. Tidying up before lunch.

            *LENA walks towards KARIN. She looks at KARIN's hand-
            bag. Pause.*

LENA   I don't think you're supposed to be doing that.

KARIN   I wasn't... I...

LENA   I don't think Hermann would be happy that/

KARIN   I'm not/

LENA   you're going through the files and/

KARIN   I don't know what you think/

LENA   taking papers/

KARIN   I'm doing, but I'm/

LENA   putting them in your handbag/

KARIN   not… doing anything/

LENA   and taking them out of the office!

> *Beat. KARIN pulls the envelope out of her handbag.*

KARIN   Nothing to hide. I'm mailing it. See?

LENA   All I see is someone who seems nervous.

KARIN   You snuck up on me!

LENA   You're hiding things.

KARIN   You're delusional.

LENA   Really? Let me take the envelope then.

KARIN   Here. Be my guest. It needs to be mailed today.

> *KARIN hands the envelope over. LENA takes it and looks at it. It appears to be addressed. She loses interest. KARIN takes the vial of sand from her purse and looks at it briefly.*

LENA   What is that?

> *She stashes the vial quickly.*

KARIN   What?

                LENA watches KARIN. Beat.

LENA   You are so lost.

KARIN   I'm not.

LENA   You are.

KARIN   I'm not—I don't know what you think you know about it anyway. I'm not you.

LENA   No. *(beat)* You're better than me, aren't you?

KARIN   I didn't mean/

LENA   Because you're in love.

KARIN   I wasn't saying/

LENA   Because he's not married.

KARIN   I was just trying to/

LENA   As far as you know…

                Beat.

KARIN   What?

LENA   Nothing.

KARIN   What do you mean?

LENA   Nothing...

KARIN   Why are you saying that?

LENA   What do you know about him? *(beat)* You're so lost.

KARIN   I'm not!

LENA   Really? What were you thinking about just now?

KARIN   This... invoice.

LENA takes it in her hands.

LENA   For manila envelopes.

KARIN   Yes. I was just thinking how expensive they're/

LENA   He's a catch, you know. Anyone would want him.

KARIN   Mr. Baum?

LENA   No. Only I want him. And maybe his whale of a wife. *(beat)* Your bookstore man.

KARIN   Markus.

LENA   Yes, Markus. They stray easily, you know. You should watch
            out if you want to keep him.

KARIN   You just don't understand men like him.

LENA   They're not all that different from one another.

KARIN   It's the men you get involved with, they have no ideals,
            they have no conviction… *(LENA shrugs, beat.)* I've never
            met anyone like him. Have you ever felt that you'll never
            meet the right one?

LENA   Romantic ideas about "the one" won't get you very far in
            the world.

KARIN   Out of nowhere he just shows up one day. How did it
            just "happen"?

LENA   Maybe it didn't.

KARIN   What do you mean?

LENA   Nothing.

KARIN   I don't understand.

LENA   Never mind. I'm jealous. That's all.

KARIN   He listens and cares and looks into my eyes when I tell
            him about my troubles, and he holds my hand, and touches
            my hair and… understands. He understands me.

LENA   Well, you'd better try to keep him then.

KARIN   Have you ever felt that?

LENA   Understood?

KARIN   Loved.

LENA   Neither. They're not common.

            *KARIN considers LENA. LENA fidgets, moving papers back
            and forth on the desk.*

            Is there something I can do to help? I think it would
            be better to feel useful. Less like I'm waiting around for
            attention/

KARIN   No, I have everything under control.

LENA   Please? It would... help me. Give me something to do
            while I'm waiting.

            Beat.

KARIN   Here, can you organize these invoices by date?

            *LENA enthusiastically takes the stack of paper over to
            the seating area and begins to lay them out. She begins
            to sort the papers.*

            You don't have to, it's quite dull.

LENA   It's what you do all day, isn't it?

KARIN   *(sadly)* yes.

LENA   You're right. It's not very exciting.

            LENA stacks the papers in order. Pause.

KARIN   What... what would you do for Hermann?

LENA   What would I *do*...?

KARIN   Would you do... anything for him?

LENA   Why are you asking?

KARIN   If he asked you to do something that made you... un-comfortable... would you do it?

LENA   This might be getting good.

KARIN   Never mind. It doesn't matter.

LENA   Has he asked you for something that makes you uncomfortable? For something... special?

KARIN   It's not/

LENA   The best way to handle that is to show a little resistance at first, like you've never heard of *that* before, like it's new, like it's a surprise, the first time/

KARIN   But it would be and I'm not talking about/

LENA   Be a bit girlish, even a bit frightened, but when it really comes down to it, show some enthusiasm for giving him what he wants.

KARIN   Oh.

LENA   So what did he ask for?

KARIN   Nothing. I don't want to/

LENA   You brought it up.

KARIN   I shouldn't have.

LENA   Suit yourself.

LENA continues to sort the papers.

KARIN   Did... Mr. Baum... did he tell you that he was married?

LENA   He's wearing a ring, darling, isn't he?

KARIN   Oh. And you still...

LENA   In case you haven't looked around recently it's difficult out there. Competitive. You don't see them? They're younger than you are. More stylish. Better looking. *(glancing at KARIN)* Darling, let's face reality. *(beat)* Hermann Baum is... appreciative. He has a good job. I know where he is most of the time. Where is Markus?

KARIN   He's... away...

LENA   Away?

KARIN   He... works abroad. He has to be away.

LENA   Of course.

KARIN   What are you implying?

LENA   Nothing.

KARIN   He loves me.

LENA   Yes. *(sardonically)* It's "magic."

KARIN   You don't know/

LENA   Maybe I don't know anything about magic. You're right.
            I know about real life. About what to wear and how to
            move and how to smell to get a man who will pay at-
            tention to me for longer than, what? You've been seeing
            him how long—a few months? I know about how to
            keep getting what I need.

KARIN   You need to hang around waiting for him to come out
            of his office? That's what you need?

LENA   That's... I... Here.

            She throws the invoices down on KARIN's desk.

Enjoy them. Enjoy your life.

LENA collects herself and grandly sweeps herself up to leave.

KARIN   No, Lena, I apologize. Don't tell Mr. Baum. I don't know what's wrong with me…

Beat. LENA turns back.

LENA   You're lost, darling. You are so lost. Don't come crying to me when he doesn't come back from one of those "business trips" some day.

LENA takes the envelope to be mailed and waves good-bye with it as she exits.

KARIN picks up her handbag and meets MARKUS.

16. Breakup

MARKUS and KARIN enter KARIN's apartment.

MARKUS   I'm glad that you're carrying the handbag. It means a lot to me. That dinner was fantastic! It's so good to be back and get some great food! And to see you, of course.

He hugs her, she disengages, hangs up her coat or places her handbag on a table. Awkward pause.

Karin?

KARIN   Hmm?

MARKUS   Am I a bore? You seem… far away.

> *KARIN can't settle, walks around the room. Pause.*

Is everything okay? Because I get the feeling that all through dinner… something is… *(beat)* Did you get my letter?

KARIN   Yes. Thank you. It was nice.

MARKUS   I wasn't sure it reached you, you didn't respond/

KARIN   No, no I got it, no problem.

MARKUS   Good.

> *Awkward pause.*

KARIN   Markus… I…

MARKUS   What is it?

KARIN   I… I don't think this is working out.

> *Beat.*

MARKUS   *(quietly)* What?

KARIN   I think... I don't think...

MARKUS   What do you mean?

KARIN   This situation, it's making me... uncomfortable.

MARKUS   We can pull back, we can/

KARIN   This is too intense, and too difficult/

MARKUS   What is? We can take it slower/

KARIN   No, my work situation, it's getting more challenging. You're away all the time, and it's just too hard... I don't think that I'm what you need.

MARKUS   This is crazy! What are you talking about, everything was fine, we went for dinner, and all of a sudden you're... Karin, don't do this/

KARIN   It's natural that with being apart, that there will be... others...

MARKUS   Is there someone else? Karin?

KARIN   No, I meant that you'll want... companionship... and I can't handle, can't sit here imagining... when I should be paying attention to what I'm doing, to the life I've built here/

MARKUS   What are you talking about?

KARIN   You want too much from me.

MARKUS I told you we can take it slow, that it doesn't have to be/

KARIN   I'm not... comfortable... with all of this. It will be easier this way.

MARKUS Easier? No. No, this isn't going to happen.

KARIN   I'm sorry.

MARKUS No. You're not, because this isn't going to happen.

        Pause.

        Don't do this.

KARIN   You should go.

MARKUS No! I'm not leaving, not until/

KARIN   Markus, this is going to be for the best. Better to do it now. You should go.

MARKUS Karin...

        KARIN moves towards the door and tries to open it. MARKUS holds it closed.

        You're making a mistake. A big mistake.

KARIN   You need someone else.

MARKUS   I need you. I guess you don't need me.

> *KARIN lets go of the door. MARKUS lets go of the door.*
> *Beat. MARKUS opens the door and exits. KARIN sits on the*
> *bed, stunned. She stares for a long moment before reach-*
> *ing for the phone, picking it up, and dialing.*
>
> *LENA appears and puts a record on the record player.*

17. Survival

> *Gloria Gaynor's "I Will Survive" plays. LENA dances.*
> *She stands on KARIN's couch, singing along. KARIN is sit-*
> *ting on the floor, curled in a defensive position with her*
> *back against the furniture. KARIN clutches the handbag*
> *that MARKUS gave her.*

LENA   C'mon. You'll feel better.

> *KARIN resists. LENA gets down on the floor with KARIN.*
> *She hands her another drink.*

Here. Drink this. You'll feel better. *(beat)* Well, you'll feel
worse. Then better.

KARIN   When?

LENA   Soon, darling. Soon.

KARIN   I don't believe you.

LENA   I know.

             Beat. KARIN drinks.

KARIN   I shouldn't have called you. I didn't know who else... I
             don't have any friends here...

             LENA turns the music down.

LENA   I'm your *friend*?

KARIN   Uh. Sure. I guess...

LENA   I don't... women don't... I don't know.

KARIN   Don't what?

LENA   Like me. I think. I don't know.

KARIN   I didn't have friends before either... didn't need them, I
             just worked and came home, worked and came home...

             KARIN loses her composure.

LENA   Don't worry, you're not alone. I'm here. What about your
             family?

KARIN   Can't. My mother… she hasn't forgiven me for leaving for Bonn behind her back. She had… plans… I couldn't live up to.

LENA   Brothers and sisters?

KARIN   There's only me. I thought maybe, someday, I'd have my own family, and it would be… but maybe not.

LENA   But maybe.

KARIN   Did I… did I make a mistake?

LENA   *(patting her like a dog)* I'm sure you did the right thing.

         LENA turns up the volume on "I Will Survive" again.

KARIN   Shut it off! Shut it off! No more!

LENA   I've always wanted a girlfriend, you know. The kind like in the movies, where you have sleepovers and talk about men and do each others' hair.

KARIN   Don't touch my hair.

LENA   No. Of course. It's just… Why didn't you have friends?

KARIN   I don't know. I just… didn't fit.

         Beat.

LENA   Do you trust me?

KARIN   What?

LENA   Do you trust me?

KARIN   I guess. Why?

LENA   It's important. I think it's important.

KARIN   Sure. But I might trust the wrong people.

            Beat.

LENA   Why did you do it?

KARIN   He… before he came here I had an important job, re-
            sponsibilities, but then I saw what he does, and nothing
            seemed as important anymore. He's away all the time,
            and instead of paying attention to what's in front of me,
            I spend my time thinking about him, who he's with, what
            he's doing, if he's thinking of me…

LENA   You been dumped before?

KARIN   I don't see what that has to do/

LENA   Many times?

KARIN   Just once.

LENA   And the other times?

KARIN   Just once. I think that's enough. Once is enough.

LENA   Sure. What's the story?

KARIN   Nothing. *(noticing the time)* I have to get to work! I have
           to be there in half an hour.

LENA   You can't go. Look at you. I'll tell Hermann.

KARIN   I have to. I have the keys, and I have to take these files
           in/

LENA   I'll take them.

KARIN   You'd do that?

LENA   Sure. You need to sleep. Come here.

> *LENA moves KARIN onto the couch. KARIN curls around
> the handbag. As LENA tucks her in she wrests the hand-
> bag from KARIN's grasp. She moves away and looks at
> the bag with interest, opening it to look at the contents.
> As she does so a paper airplane flies in through the win-
> dow. LENA looks out the window. LENA opens the paper
> airplane and reads what's written on it. She considers,
> then presses it flat before leaving it and the handbag
> beside a napping KARIN.*

Karin? You did the right thing.

LENA picks up the office keys and documents that need to be delivered. The scene shifts. KARIN picks herself up and despondently moves to her desk at the ministry.

20. Togetherness

The Federal Ministry of Economics. KARIN is at her desk. LENA enters. She pauses, conflicted, before speaking.

LENA   He's outside.

KARIN   Who is?

LENA   Guess.

KARIN goes back to her work.

Aren't you going to go and see him? How many letters has he sent you? One a day? Just go out and talk to him. He looks pathetic.

KARIN   I'm working.

LENA   I... I'll cover for you.

KARIN reluctantly puts on her coat and goes outside to meet MARKUS, who is standing, shivering in the cold, on the sidewalk.

MARKUS   Thanks for coming out.

KARIN   What do you want?

MARKUS   I've been sending you letters. You haven't replied.

KARIN   No, I haven't.

MARKUS   Karin, look, I've tried to just walk away, to forget about
            you. I can't. And you can't make me believe that you don't
            want to be with me too.

KARIN   I… you should stop sending letters.

            Long pause.

MARKUS   Are you happy? *(beat)* I didn't think so. What do you
            want to hear?

KARIN   I don't know.

MARKUS   What do you want?

KARIN   I don't know.

MARKUS   Then maybe it's possible you want what we already have.
            (beat) I think about you all the time. I'm supposed to be
            handing out food aid, and deciding who gets what rations,
            and I can't think straight because I remember being with
            you on the beach in Bulgaria, or at the restaurant the time
            we spent the whole night laughing, or in your bed…

MARKUS reaches for her.

KARIN   Don't…

MARKUS embraces her anyway. She softens.

MARKUS   You can't tell me you haven't missed this.

Pause. They stay in the embrace for the moment.

We can make it anything we want it to be, right? We can take it slower, if you're not comfortable/

KARIN   I have missed you. I'd need to take it slower/

MARKUS   moving so quickly, then/

KARIN   I get overwhelmed, I just/

MARKUS   we can do it a bit at a time/

KARIN   get frightened. This is difficult/

MARKUS   work our way up to it/

KARIN   for me.

Beat.

I love you.

MARKUS   I know. I love you too.

KARIN   We can take it slow?

MARKUS   Slow as you want, take as much time as you want.

KARIN   I've thought about you too. Every day. I'm sorry.

MARKUS   It doesn't matter now. Lena tell you I was out here?

KARIN   Yes.

MARKUS   Good.

KARIN   I don't think she'll be happy about it though.

MARKUS   Why's that?

KARIN   She was telling me to burn the letters, not to read them.

MARKUS   Really.

KARIN   I think she was trying to protect me.

MARKUS   From me?

KARIN   Maybe from myself.

MARKUS   Doesn't matter now.

KARIN   We'll take it slow?

MARKUS   I promise.

> *The scene shifts. LENA appears in a pastel bridesmaid's dress and helps KARIN into a wedding dress.*

22. *Wedding*

> *The "Wedding March" begins. A sunny day on the beach. The perfect wedding day. Birds chirp, waves gently roll into the shore. Everyone is beautiful.*

> *LENA comes directly downstage to the audience in her bridesmaid's dress. MARKUS appears in a suit. KARIN turns and walks down the aisle.*

> *Pause. MARKUS and KARIN smile, look at the audience, look at each other. Pause. They kiss. The sun sets.*

> *Pachelbel's* Canon in D *begins. LENA hugs the both of them to her tightly.*

> *MARKUS and LENA help KARIN out of her wedding dress. They take it offstage. KARIN turns, smiles, getting down to work.*

24. An Ending

KARIN cleans her apartment. She opens the door to LENA, who is crying.

KARIN   Come in. What's/

LENA   He's leaving me!

KARIN   Mr. Baum? Why?

LENA   I'm so…

KARIN   What happened?

LENA   You're busy.

KARIN   Just unpacking some more boxes. Can you believe it's been almost six months since the wedding, and I still haven't… never mind. That doesn't matter.

LENA   Markus is away?

KARIN   Yes.

LENA   Where this time?

KARIN   He couldn't say. Confidential.

LENA   Have you heard from him?

KARIN   It's been… weeks. I'm getting worried. I don't know…

LENA   Weeks since you've heard from him? Why?

KARIN   I don't know.

LENA   Do you think he's okay/

KARIN   I don't know!

LENA   But what could/

KARIN   What about Mr. Baum, what happened?

LENA   He was… asking me these questions. Angry. He was yelling at me. You don't… you won't hate me, will you?

KARIN   Why? What are you/

LENA   He thought that I… I did it. He told me to get out, but I… I'm so sorry.

KARIN   Sorry for what? Lena, you aren't making any sense.

LENA   He thought that I… took things.

KARIN   What?

LENA   That I took documents.

KARIN   Why would he think that?

LENA   I don't know. I don't know, I think things are missing. I
            had to. Hermann thought it was me.

KARIN   *(warning)* Lena…

LENA   I'm… *(She sniffles.)* What am I supposed to do now?

KARIN   He can't really believe you've done that. I'm sure it will
            work out.

LENA   In your world it does. When it's all pre-arranged.

KARIN   What are you talking about?

            A loud and scary knocking at the door. Again, persistent.

LENA   I'm sorry.

KARIN   Why?

            Knocking again, louder.

LENA   They're here to arrest you.

            *KARIN attempts to walk across the room to the door. Her
            legs seem rubbery, as if they are getting away from her.
            They give way and she collapses onto the floor.*

            *LENA stands up sharply, goes to look at KARIN on the
            floor, as if she might help her, then steps past, towards
            the door. She opens it.*

She's in here.

Snap to black

End Act I.

ACT II
A LOVE STORY?

Act II is solid and industrial in look and feel.

1. Black Sea Coast

The sound of waves crashing onto a beach. Soothing.

A woman, KARIN, in her thirties, dressed smartly, sits at a bistro table near the Black Sea. She is reading a book, looking up occasionally to admire the sun setting over the waves. There is coffee in a fine cup in front of her.

The sound of the waves increases. She pauses, puts down her book, and sips her coffee, then picks up the book again and continues reading.

A good-looking man in a good-quality suit, in his late thirties or early forties, enters tentatively. He walks across the stage, looking for someone. There is no one. He crosses the length of the stage, looks offstage, at a loss, wanders back again. He stands uncertainly. The woman notices.

The man sees the woman watching him and acknowledges her, embarrassed to have attracted attention. He continues to stand and twitch. Very long pause.

The man looks for a place to sit. There is only the extra chair at the bistro table. The woman sees him regard the chair. They both look at the chair intently. Finally she looks at him and shrugs. He takes the chair nervously and sits. Pause. Shift to:

2. Psych Meeting #1

MARKUS stands in a spotlight. Lights come up on a row of chairs upstage, arranged in a slight semicircle behind him. The empty chairs are the psychological team and remain in place throughout the act. He addresses them as if they were in front of him. MARKUS holds a manila file and a notebook that he refers to occasionally.

MARKUS   Target was approached seaside on the appointed date. Appeared to be interested, especially when Stuttgart and opera were mentioned, and seemed to enjoy being nurturing. *(switching to notebook)* Initial information was imparted, including: hometown of Stuttgart, mother in opera, legend of international humanitarian work. She reached out to touch me two... no, three... times during the encounter, and at one point nearly propositioned me to a night in her hotel room. Believe she lost her nerve to go through with the idea.

Did place "false time constraint" as instructed, and left the scene without giving the target hope of a future meeting.

As described, target does appear to be isolated, lonely, and vulnerable. And importantly… idealistic.

(pause, looks up as he receives instructions) Yes. Yes, I have received the next assignment. Travel is booked. Have received photographs of previous lover who jilted target, and will attempt similar grooming techniques. Thank you for the opportunity to serve the party.

> *Lights shift.*

3. Bookstore

> *MARKUS stands, leaning against a wall or post. Bored. He looks at his watch, watches people on the street, looks at his watch again. Looks at his notebook.*

> *KARIN enters and walks by into the bookstore. MARKUS sees her, looks at his watch, and appears to count out the time before following her into the bookstore.*

> *MARKUS appears to browse. KARIN notices him. She starts to approach him, then thinks better of it, losing her nerve. She gains confidence and reapproaches.*

KARIN   Markus?

MARKUS   Yes?

KARIN   I thought it was you! What are you doing in Bonn?

MARKUS   Pardon, I... oh! Oh, it's you.

KARIN   Uh... yes. Karin.

MARKUS   I didn't recognize you.

KARIN   I guess it's different without the/

MARKUS   Sand. The sea.

KARIN   Not so much of that here. It's a *dry* city. Government town.

MARKUS   Are you looking for a book? Stupid question.

KARIN   I'm always looking for a book. But what are you... this is crazy! What are the odds that I'd run into you here...

MARKUS   I know! It's... something.

KARIN   For sure, something.

        Awkward pause.

        Well... I... shouldn't interrupt/

MARKUS   Oh, no/

KARIN   I mean, it was just so strange/

MARKUS   You're not interrupting/

KARIN   seeing you here/

MARKUS   Not at all/

KARIN   I thought maybe I should/

MARKUS   It's nice to see you.

KARIN   say hello. *(beat)* Or something.

           Another awkward pause.

           Are you here for a long time, or…

MARKUS   Four days.

KARIN   *(disappointed)* Oh. *(beat)* Well, I guess I should let you
           get back to your…

MARKUS   *(looking directly into her eyes)* It really is remarkable, isn't
           it?

KARIN   Remarkable?

MARKUS   Meeting you again. Like this.

KARIN   It is…

           Pause. They look at each other.

MARKUS   *(indicating the book he's carrying)* I should…

KARIN   Right. Of course. Me too, I'm only on lunch/

MARKUS   You work close by?

KARIN   The Federal Ministry of Economics. Down the block.

MARKUS   I see. *(awkward pause)* Well, I guess I should purchase
            this and be getting back.

KARIN   Yes, me too. *(She goes to leave, turns back.)* You're working
            on something important here?

MARKUS   Trying to get some funding for a relief project in South
            America.

KARIN   Wow, that does sound interesting. Good luck with that.
            (beat, flailing) Four days?

MARKUS   Pardon?

KARIN   You're here for only four days?

MARKUS   Yes.

            Awkward pause.

KARIN   Ah. *(beat)* Well, I hope you enjoy your time here.

MARKUS   Thank you. I hope you enjoy your… lunch.

KARIN　　　Thank you.

> *Both stand and look at each other, not moving. Pause.*
> *MARKUS breaks the connection by taking his book and*
> *moving towards the cash area. KARIN exhales and vis-*
> *ibly deflates.*

> *As KARIN walks offstage she leaves glow-in-the-dark*
> *footprints behind her on the darkening stage.*

> *Lights down.*

6. *Markus's Letter*

> *MARKUS is standing in front of the semicircle of chairs,*
> *which are also lit. KARIN sits at her desk, reading his*
> *letter.*

MARKUS　　*(emotionless, robotic)* Dear Karin. I greatly enjoyed our
time together in Bonn. Actually, I… keep thinking about
you. I'm supposed to be focused on getting medical sup-
plies to the refugees here, and all I can think about is
you. Is that crazy? Probably. I've arranged to come back
to Bonn at the end of my time here. Until then, I'll sit
under these stars and imagine you here with me. Soon,
Markus.

8. *A Momentous Date*

> *MARKUS and KARIN have just entered KARIN's apartment. They're wet, it's been raining. MARKUS carries a dripping umbrella. They look at each other, unsure of what to do next.*

KARIN   Oh! I should…

> *She gestures to take his coat.*

MARKUS   *(finding a place for the umbrella and handing her his coat)*
Yes. Thank you.

> *MARKUS fidgets awkwardly by the door.*

KARIN   Would you like to come in?

MARKUS   Thank you. I like your apartment. It's very… clean.

KARIN   Thank you.

> *MARKUS stands in the middle of the room.*

Would you like to… sit?

> *MARKUS sits. KARIN sits. A pause.*

A drink?

MARKUS   Yes. That would be nice.

KARIN gets up to pour a highball.

I've really loved tonight. It's been so good to see you.

KARIN   Me too. Loved tonight.

MARKUS   I've… thought about you.

KARIN   I've thought about you too.

MARKUS   You have?

KARIN   Yes.

MARKUS   I like that.

KARIN   I'm glad.

KARIN give MARKUS his drink, sits. MARKUS downs his drink quickly. He moves closer to KARIN.

MARKUS   What have you thought about?

He touches her arm or her leg.

KARIN   Uh… seeing you?

MARKUS   Yes? I've thought about other things too.

KARIN   *(nervously)* Yes?

MARKUS   Yes.

> *He is close to her now, moving in.*

KARIN   Like… like what things?

MARKUS   Like… this…

> *He pulls her to him and kisses her forcefully.*

KARIN   Markus… I just don't know that we're… that I'm… ready…

MARKUS   Oh?

> *Long pause. He backs off. He stands up and takes his glass back to the bar area.*

Oh. That's fine. It's better this way.

KARIN   What?

MARKUS   It's probably for the best.

KARIN   What do you mean?

MARKUS   That we not get too involved. That you're being smart. It's the right decision.

KARIN   No, I/

MARKUS   I'm away with work all the time, it's always on my mind…
             I'm not a very good catch for a girl like you…

KARIN   No! Markus, I didn't mean… what's the matter? *(reach-
             ing out to him)*

                   MARKUS takes a drink. A long pause.

MARKUS   Nothing. Work.

KARIN   What is it? You can talk to me.

MARKUS   I can't… I can't find out what projects are in the area,
             who's in charge of… forget it.

KARIN   Your work is so hard on you.

MARKUS   It's my life.

                   KARIN reaches out to comfort him.

KARIN   I'm sorry.

MARKUS   Doesn't have anything to do with you/

KARIN   About just now. I… I do want to kiss you, you know.

MARKUS   You do?

KARIN   I do.

She pulls him towards her, kisses him.

MARKUS   No. No, you were right, it isn't a good idea…

KARIN   No, I was wrong, I was just/

MARKUS   Maybe we shouldn't/

KARIN   No, no I want to/

MARKUS   My schedule is out of control/

KARIN   I just wasn't sure that you/

MARKUS   Work is very important, I can't just/

KARIN   would respect me, and/

MARKUS   be thinking about someone else when/

KARIN   I didn't want you to think I was easy/

MARKUS   I should be taking care of those that need/

KARIN   No girl wants to think that she's/

MARKUS   my help/

KARIN   easy, but I/

MARKUS   I shouldn't be acting like a teenager.

KARIN   really care for you.

MARKUS   If I could only... DAMMIT!

> *Pause. KARIN reaches out to touch MARKUS.*

KARIN   I wish there was something I could do...

MARKUS   I don't want to talk anymore.

KARIN   But I know that it's bothering you/

> *KARIN reaches for him again. MARKUS pulls away. Long pause.*

I hate seeing you like this.

MARKUS   There's nothing you can do.

> *He realizes his distraction and reaches out to touch her.*

It's pointless. I shouldn't be talking about work when I'm with you.

KARIN   But you'll... you still want...

MARKUS   I do... but...

> *MARKUS starts to collect his umbrella, look for his coat.*

KARIN   If you had… If you had that information…?

MARKUS   Karin…

KARIN   I might be able to…

MARKUS   I can't ask you to…

           She approaches him, kisses him.

KARIN   You're not asking.

           She takes the umbrella away from him. Lights down.

10. Psych Meeting #2

           *MARKUS stands in the spotlight. Lights come up on the
           chairs. He addresses them as if they were in front of him.*

MARKUS   I do understand that the next stage is classified as "Inter-
           mittent Approval." My assignment now is to ensure that
           she… the target, will experience periods of validation fol-
           lowed by periods of abandonment and confusion. Time
           spent with the target will be necessarily brief and emotion-
           ally heightened through gifts, undivided attention, poetic
           expressions of love, and attentive sex. I am to follow the
           brief periods with much longer periods of no contact. This
           activity will produce feelings of doubt and insecurity and

motivate the target to strategize ways of making contact, including the turning over of sensitive documentation.

At the words "intermittent approval," lights come up on KARIN in another area of the stage. She is sitting on the floor, drinking, and staring intently at the telephone. She is despondent.

The phone rings. KARIN jumps then answers it excitedly.

KARIN   Hello? *(beat, then disappointed)* Oh.

Lights shift.

11. Documents

MARKUS stands leaning against a wall or a post. He checks his watch. LENA enters with an envelope.

LENA   Markus?

MARKUS   Yes?

LENA   Karin sent me. To give you this. She couldn't get away.

MARKUS   She asked you to…

LENA   I offered.

MARKUS   Ah.

> *LENA holds out the envelope. MARKUS goes to take it but she pulls it back.*

LENA   What is it?

MARKUS   What do you mean/

LENA   What is *this*?

MARKUS   She asked me to meet her here/

LENA   Maybe I should keep it, or open it/

> *LENA threatens to open the envelope. MARKUS reaches for it.*

           What is she giving you?

MARKUS   Papers that I forgot at her apartment.

LENA   Yes… that's what she said.

MARKUS   Papers that are for me to read. Me only.

LENA   It's good you both got the story straight.

> *Beat.*

MARKUS   She thinks you're her friend.

LENA   Maybe I am.

MARKUS   I think you're nobody's friend.

LENA   *(smiling)* I could be your friend.

> *Beat.*

MARKUS   Could you?

LENA   Yes.

> *Long pause.*

MARKUS   My friends help me. They give me what I want.

LENA   I can be very friendly.

> *MARKUS grabs for the envelope, but LENA holds it out of reach. MARKUS puts LENA into a physical lock and wrests the envelope from her, cognizant of the people who may be passing by.*

(rubbing her sore arm, smiling) Bit of a brute, aren't you?

> *MARKUS takes a long look at LENA, then exits.*

12. Psych Meeting #3

MARKUS stands in front of the psychology team.

MARKUS It is going well. Karin… the target, has the handbag and the recording device is active. Recording quality is not very good, and nothing useful has been acquired through this means to date. We will continue to monitor in case something of value should be recorded.

Yes… it's true. Hermann Baum's mistress has expressed… interest… in me and is getting too close to the work I'm doing. I'm concerned that she… Sorry…? I don't mean to disagree with your expert opinions, but I think that action would be detrimental…

No, I'm not trying to be difficult, I just don't… I think it will cause unnecessary harm to her/ *(He catches himself.)* the target, should the situation…

A pause while he listens. He straightens himself and gains his composure.

Yes. I will engage the secondary target. *(beat)* It's just that/

He's interrupted. Beat.

Of course. Done. Thank you for the opportunity to serve the party.

MARKUS, tense, acknowledges the team, then exits.

13. Lena

A small rented room. LENA lounges on the bed with few clothes on. MARKUS gets dressed.

LENA   Don't go.

MARKUS   It's time to go. It's time for you to go too.

LENA   *(pouting)* But I don't want to…

MARKUS   C'mon. Time to go.

LENA   But don't you want this?

> *She holds up an envelope. When he gets near, she hides it behind her back. He refuses to play the game, then relents, kissing her roughly and taking it from her at the same time.*

You're welcome. *(beat)* You don't do aid work, do you? *(no answer)* I don't care, you know. It doesn't matter to me one way or the other.

MARKUS   It's an important cause.

LENA   And I'm helping?

MARKUS   Yes.

LENA   Isn't that nice of me. *(beat)* You know, I could do with a little romance.

> *MARKUS laughs. He gathers his items up and puts them in his briefcase, tidies the room, throws LENA's clothes to her.*

(wounded) What? Is that so hard to imagine?

MARKUS   Not your style.

LENA   I'm no different than any other woman. We all want to be romanced, loved, seduced… why is it so hard to believe that maybe I'd want that? You dish up the charm for her.

MARKUS   That's different.

LENA   Why?

MARKUS   It's time for you to get going.

> *LENA sees something by the bed. She picks up a jar with KARIN's underwear in it.*

LENA   WHAT is this??

> *MARKUS tries to grab it from her, but she plays keep away.*

What… is this HERS? Is it? What kind of a pervert… Why the hell have you got her underwear?? And you have it just SITTING there, sitting there when you're with me! Are you thinking about that MOUSE when you're/

MARKUS   Lena, enough!!

LENA   Then why the hell haven't you asked for mine? Why her,
              why... tell me what it's for, tell me/

              She tries to open the jar.

MARKUS   Don't!

              *MARKUS and LENA fight for ownership of the jar. MARKUS
              wins by overpowering her.*

              No questions. Or we can't meet anymore.

LENA   You think you're so special to me?

MARKUS   Those are the rules, I'm just repeating them.

LENA   *(mocking)* "No questions." *(beat)* What if I tell her? What
              would happen then? What would Miss Mouse do then?

MARKUS   You're not going to do that.

LENA   Why not?

              LENA starts to dress.

MARKUS   *(grabbing her arm)* I'm not an old man who is going to
              give in to your childish whining.

LENA   I don't see why you can't break it off with her. You have
              me, you don't need/

MARKUS   *(He softens.)* Lena, come here. *(He pulls her onto his lap.)*
           You and I… we understand each other. We connect on
           a level that's… deep. You feel that, right? *(LENA nods.)*
           We get what we need from each other.

               LENA softens, curls up to him, childlike.

           There. Perfect. When we're like this we can be happy.
           And I don't have to tell Hermann that you're going be-
           hind his back, and you don't have to tell/

LENA   You wouldn't!

MARKUS   I don't think you'd have a lot of visitors in jail. I've got
           your fingerprints all over sensitive documentation that
           you've handed over.

LENA   But… but you'd be turning over yourself/

MARKUS   No, that part is easy. Lots of ways to get the information
           where it needs to be.

LENA   But I just did it so that you'd/

MARKUS   So, we have an understanding.

LENA   I just don't see why you need her anymore. Why can't
           you just be with me, I can get you what you need/

MARKUS   Time to leave.

LENA   Wait. Just wait a moment.

            *LENA embraces MARKUS tightly. She looks up into his
            eyes.*

            Do you know that sharks, when they're about to bite
            something, have a film that goes over their eyes so they
            can't see what they're biting.

            MARKUS starts to pull her off of him.

            Men have this look, I've seen it.

            *LENA pulls herself tighter to MARKUS. She places her
            head over his heart.*

MARKUS   Why do you always do that?

LENA   I can hear your heart. It can't lie, it always tells the truth.

            MARKUS disentangles himself from her.

MARKUS   You have half an hour. I'll be back, and you have to be
            gone by then.

            MARKUS exits.

LENA   And maybe you don't see me. But you will.

            Lights shift.

15. Karin's Second Letter

KARIN is sitting on the floor. MARKUS is reading her letter. The chairs behind him are lit.

KARIN   *(distraught)* Dear Markus. Will this letter reach you? I haven't heard from you in two weeks. Please come home. I need to feel your arms around me. Where are you? I hope you are safe. And thinking of me.

Lights shift. Focus on MARKUS.

18. Psych Meeting #4

MARKUS, agitated, stands in front of the psychology team.

MARKUS   I don't know what happened! It was going well, she was regularly turning over minor documents and seemed open to the idea of escalating the situation but... *(getting frustrated)* I don't KNOW. I had no indication that she was doubting the relationship, that she was going to end it...

My attention has been split by the secondary objective you've saddled me with! It's difficult to keep it all... yes. I apologize. I am listening.

This is NOT a failure, it… I underestimated her reluctance to commit, or allowed the intermittent periods to go on for too long…

Yes. Yes, it's possible that I can do that. I AM capable of… I think I know the target better than…

A pause while he listens. He straightens himself and gains composure.

Yes. I will perform as directed. Thank you for the opportunity to serve the party.

MARKUS, tense, acknowledges the team, then exits.

19. Reconciliation

KARIN lies on her bed. A paper airplane arrives. She reads it.

MARKUS   Karin, these last few weeks without you have been unbearable. The thought of never seeing you again haunts me. You can't believe that this is the best decision for us, because I know that this is a mistake. I will write you every day. I will not give up on us. I love you. Markus.

21. Proposal

Moonlit night, a beach. MARKUS and KARIN are dressed for the opera they have just attended. They walk languorously along the edge of the water.

KARIN   So this is what you were planning.

MARKUS   Yes.

KARIN   Opera and a moonlit beach. That's quite an evening.

MARKUS   Yes. Did you like it? The opera?

KARIN   It was beautiful. Breathtaking. Although sad…

MARKUS   You can't expect *Romeo and Juliet* to turn out with a happy ending.

KARIN   I suppose not. But somehow you still hope for them. I don't know why that is. You know how it will end, and still… you feel for them.

MARKUS   Love doesn't change, I suppose. Centuries later it's the same.

KARIN   A bit of magic…

MARKUS   A bit of magic all arranged.

MARKUS takes KARIN's hand. They listen to the waves.

KARIN   Ah… the water… that's why we're here, isn't it?

MARKUS   Restorative. Do you remember?

KARIN   Meeting you? No, I've forgotten all about it.

            Pause.

MARKUS   Karin, I'm glad you reconsidered. Being back together
            has been so wonderful that…

KARIN   We're a good team.

MARKUS   We are. Here, take those shoes off.

            *He takes her shoes off and then his. He drags his feet
            through the sand, making figures.*

            Feel that? Nothing like the cool sand, the smell of this
            place. Look at your lovely, lovely toes.

KARIN   They're frog-like.

MARKUS   And I love them. The sand feels so wonderful…

            He finishes moving his toes deliberately in the sand.

            See… look.

KARIN   What...?

MARKUS   I brought you here to ask you this question.

KARIN   Markus!

            MARKUS drops to his knees.

MARKUS   Will you marry me?

KARIN   I... Yes! Yes I'll marry you!

            They kiss.

MARKUS   I love you.

KARIN   I love you too. How did you hold that in all night?

MARKUS   *(teasing)* It's a talent.

KARIN   I can hardly wait... When can we have the wedding? It
            doesn't have to be fancy, I don't mind at all, I/

MARKUS   We may have to... wait a while.

KARIN   What? Why?

MARKUS   Things are... difficult... now.

KARIN   Markus?

MARKUS   Don't worry, lovely. It will all be fine. It just might take
          a little while to… sort things out.

KARIN   How long? *(no answer)* Markus?

          He doesn't answer and hugs her to him.

MARKUS   Look at the moon. It's just for us tonight.

          Beat.

KARIN   Can I help?

MARKUS   I don't know/

KARIN   Markus, we're a team. We're in this together. What do
          you need?

MARKUS   More… difficult to obtain information. From other of-
          fices you have access to.

KARIN   But how would I/

MARKUS   You have the security access and you'd just need to copy
          the documents/

KARIN   I could be caught, what would/

MARKUS   No one will suspect you. You're trusted. A secretary. You
          stumbled into the wrong area. Mr. Baum asked you for
          something and you're trying to locate it…

KARIN   But I'm risking myself.

             *Pause. MARKUS turns away. Beat. KARIN reaches out to
             try to touch him.*

             You risk yourself every day, don't you?

MARKUS   *(turning)* You know why this is important. Lives de-
             pend on it. I'm just so… there's only so much I can do
             to help these people, and these bureaucrats block every
             attempt/

KARIN   It's just… if we're caught, what happens/

MARKUS   Never mind. I should never have brought it up…

             He pulls her to him fiercely.

             I just wanted to let you know what was going on, why
             we might have to wait.

             MARKUS and KARIN embrace.

KARIN   Oh… the water is already taking it away…

MARKUS   Doesn't matter.

KARIN   But I wish I could keep it forever.

MARKUS   All of that is an illusion. This is real.

KARIN   And forever.

MARKUS   …forever…

> *The lights fade down.*

22. Wedding

Mendelssohn's "Wedding March" begins.

It's raining. LENA tries to help KARIN with her dress. LENA holds an umbrella over her. The wedding is reversed from Act I, so that the audience is seeing "backstage." LENA goes directly upstage, through a row created through the middle of the psychological team. MARKUS appears upstage in a suit.

Pause. MARKUS and KARIN kiss.

Pachelbel's Canon in D *begins. LENA hugs the both of them to her tightly. LENA turns, and as she does, her umbrella moves to cover MARKUS and herself, leaving KARIN in the rain. LENA kisses MARKUS meaningfully. KARIN doesn't notice.*

23. Psych Meeting #5

MARKUS stands in front of the psychology team. He begins to pace, agitated.

MARKUS   I feel an obligation to follow through with my promises. I... struggle... with this situation... Is that a threat...? Well maybe you didn't do your profiling well enough. You can't ask me to do what you're asking...

You can ask. But I won't do it. What will you do to me? What CAN you do to me!?

Lights shift quickly.

24. An Ending

KARIN cleans her apartment. She opens the door to LENA, who is crying.

KARIN   Come in. What's/

LENA   Markus is away?

KARIN   Yes.

LENA   Where this time?

KARIN   He couldn't say. Confidential.

LENA   Have you heard from him?

KARIN   It's been... weeks. I'm getting worried. I don't know...

LENA   Weeks since you've heard from him? Why?

KARIN   I don't know.

LENA   Do you think he's okay/

KARIN   I don't know!

LENA   But what could...

KARIN   Come and sit/

LENA   I'm so sorry.

KARIN   Sorry for what? Lena, you aren't making any sense.

          A loud and scary knocking at the door. Again, persistent.

LENA   I'm sorry.

KARIN   Why?

          Knocking again, louder.

LENA   They're here to arrest you.

KARIN attempts to walk across the room to the door. Her legs seem rubbery, as if they are getting away from her. They give way and she collapses onto the floor.

LENA stands up sharply, goes to look at KARIN on the floor, as if she might help her, then steps past, towards the door. She opens it.

She's in here.

End Act II.

Sound of a heavy jail door sliding and closing.

ACT III
A STORY

Act III is cold and sparse in look and feel.

25. Reunion

Six months later. KARIN is in a sparse apartment that has a table and chairs and little else. It is harshly lit. She is simply dressed. She puts out the things for coffee. A briefcase is also in the room. She appears a bit agitated.

A loud knock at the door. KARIN jumps. She opens the door. LENA is there, dressed elegantly in black.

KARIN   Hello.

LENA   Hello.

KARIN   Can I take your...?

LENA   Yes. Thanks.

        Awkward pause.

KARIN   Coffee? *(She gestures to the table.)*

LENA   Thank you.

LENA sits. KARIN pours.

This place…

KARIN   I know. It isn't much.

LENA   No, no, it's fine. I'm sure you'll make something of it.

KARIN   It isn't easy to find a place when…

LENA   Yes. I can imagine.

          Awkward pause.

I was surprised to see you yesterday.

KARIN   I didn't expect to see you there/

LENA   I couldn't let him go without saying goodbye.

KARIN   You're still in black?

LENA   Oh, this? I just like it.

KARIN   Oh.

LENA   I think it's quite elegant really. Don't know why I don't wear black more often.

KARIN   It suits you.

          LENA looks at KARIN sharply. She drinks.

LENA   Have you been out long...?

KARIN   A few weeks.

LENA   I thought your sentence/

KARIN   Good behaviour.

LENA   Ah.

KARIN   Yes, I'm a model prisoner it seems. Out in six months.

LENA   You're good at everything you try.

KARIN   As are you.

LENA   *(not sure how to take the barb)* ...Yes...

KARIN   I read it was a heart attack.

LENA   I wouldn't know.

KARIN   You weren't still...?

LENA   Oh, yes, but I wasn't with him when it happened. Hermann was an old man, something was bound to happen sooner or later.

KARIN   Still, sad to see Mr. Baum pass on.

LENA   His wife seemed upset.

KARIN   I guess that might be expected.

LENA   Yes, I suppose.

KARIN   She didn't seem pleased to see you.

LENA   They usually aren't.

          Beat.

KARIN   Thanks for coming.

LENA   Sure... I was surprised that you asked me to visit.

KARIN   I thought maybe... I don't know.

LENA   Thought what?

KARIN   That you might... have answers, I guess. I've gone over and
          over every detail in my mind, everything that happened...
          I've had nothing else to do for the last six months, and it
          doesn't add up.

LENA   I know. It's shocking. Let's just focus on now. Forget
          about that.

KARIN   I just thought we could discuss/

LENA   And concentrate/

KARIN   what had happened/

LENA   on what's here and now/

KARIN   because I feel like I need to/

LENA   Like the fact that I'm engaged!

> *LENA shows KARIN her ring. Beat.*

KARIN   Oh. It's… congratulations.

LENA   Thank you! I'm thrilled to bits.

KARIN   It must be wonderful/

LENA   After all this time, I've finally found Prince Charming.

KARIN   That's… wonderful.

LENA   It really is, isn't it.

> *Pause.*

KARIN   I was really hoping that/

LENA   Listen, Karin, I don't want to talk about that.

KARIN   But I don't see why we can't discuss it, it's important to
               me, and I think you owe it to me.

LENA   I *owe* you?

KARIN   No, I meant that/

LENA   For telling the police the truth about what you were doing?

KARIN   I didn't know/

LENA   Come on. You're not really that stupid.

KARIN   I didn't. You were there!

LENA   You'd have to be pretty dim-witted/

KARIN   So I deserved it, that's what you're saying?

LENA   I'm not saying anything. *(beat)* Listen, I didn't want to talk about this because I knew it would upset you.

KARIN   What about the documents you turned over?

LENA   *(quietly)* What?

KARIN   The documents you took from me and delivered to Markus.

LENA   *(relieved)* Oh. That. Well, obviously that had nothing to do with me, you told me they were documents that already belonged to him.

KARIN   And the others.

LENA   Others?

KARIN   More coffee?

                 A loud knock at the door. Both women jump.

LENA   *(checking her watch)* That's probably my fiancé. I asked
                 him to come by and pick me up/

KARIN   Need to leave so soon?

LENA   *(gathering her things)* I didn't realize how... angry... you
                 are. It's not a good look.

                 Another knock. KARIN answers the door. MARKUS is there.
                 They are stunned to see each other. Long pause.

MARKUS   I... is Lena...?

LENA   Darling, I was just telling Karin about the engagement.

MARKUS   Karin, I didn't know you were...

KARIN   Out of jail?

MARKUS   No, I mean, yes, I...

KARIN   Or having coffee with your fiancé. Coffee's still hot. Have
                 a seat.

MARKUS   I don't think/

KARIN   A few minutes. We can catch up.

MARKUS   We should be/

KARIN   *(forcefully)* Sit.

> MARKUS *does.* LENA *sits beside him, touching his arm, fixing his shirt.* MARKUS *looks around the room nervously, suspiciously.* KARIN *pours coffee.*

                You're getting married.

LENA   Next month.

KARIN   Summer. How nice.

LENA   If we'd known you were… out… we might have invited you.

KARIN   Here in Bonn?

LENA   No, abroad.

KARIN   Black Sea coast?

LENA   *(confused)* No, why…

MARKUS   We need to go.

KARIN   Only thing is… I don't think you can get married.

LENA   Why is that?

KARIN   Because you're still married to me. Officially. Or had you forgotten that part?

Markus gets up and looks out the window nervously.

LENA   Tell her.

MARKUS   I won't sit here and be used like a/

KARIN   Tell me what?

MARKUS   playtoy between the two of you.

LENA   *Tell her.*

Markus stares at Lena stonily.

You're not really married.

KARIN   *(to Markus)* What?

MARKUS   Goddammit!

KARIN   What are you talking about?

MARKUS   It's true.

KARIN   But... I was there... you were there... we... Christ, even
she was there/

MARKUS   I don't know what to say, Karin.

LENA   It was a set-up.

KARIN   Set-up?

LENA   Tell her.

KARIN   I think you owe it to me/

LENA   There's that "owing" again, that's getting old/

MARKUS   They were agents. The minister, the guests from my side…

KARIN   Your father?

        Beat.

MARKUS   My supervisor. *(to LENA)* Are you done now?

LENA   I think the question is is she done. She seems to have
            some… issues surrounding you, love. Things that need
            to be set straight.

KARIN   Yes, I need to be set straight.

LENA   She needs to know the difference between fairy tales and
            what's real.

KARIN   Fairy tales?

LENA   The difference between following orders and choosing
            love.

        Beat.

KARIN   Does she know?

MARKUS   Know what?

KARIN   Does she?

LENA   I'm not as dull as you are.

KARIN   Really?

LENA   I knew from the start.

KARIN   The very beginning?

LENA   Sure. Not hard to figure out. You're just not smart. You
           don't see things. You don't know how the world works.

KARIN   And you do?

LENA   I told you. I know how to get what I want.

KARIN   *(looking at MARKUS)* Obviously. You're right. You win.

LENA   Markus and I are the perfect team. I got him exactly
           what he wanted. I didn't hesitate, I went straight for the
           best—"secret" and "top secret" papers/

MARKUS   Lena!

KARIN   So, unlike me you knew what you were doing by turning
           over those documents.

LENA   Of course I did.

KARIN   Because you're smarter than I am.

LENA   That's right.

KARIN   But *Markus*, I'm still confused then. Why did you keep
          seeing me, "marry me," for whatever that's worth, when
          you already had your "team"? You were together before
          we were married, right?

LENA   You weren't married!

MARKUS   Karin, I was under orders… I'm not having this conver-
          sation.

KARIN   Needed to carry my panties with you even after/

LENA   He didn't need you!

MARKUS   Karin, I can explain, they wanted "smell samples" on file,
          it wasn't/

LENA   You needed her "smell sample"?

KARIN   I think I deserve/

LENA   You deserve nothing!

MARKUS   Lena, that's enough! Leave her alone.

LENA   Leave her alone? Why?

MARKUS   She's been through enough, you don't need to/

LENA   Don't tell me what I do or do not need to do!

MARKUS   Enough!

LENA   You can't tell me what to do. You don't *own* me/

KARIN   A match made in heaven.

LENA   Shut up, mouse! You were in over your head to begin
              with, to think that he could possibly care for you/

MARKUS   Lena!

KARIN   Or anyone. Do you think he could care for anyone, Lena?
              Or are you just convenient, maybe? Now that Hermann
              is gone, where will you get the information from?

LENA   That's, he's… we're not just together because…

KARIN   That's right. You love her. Go on, tell her, *Markus. (beat)*
              Does she know?

LENA   He chose me.

KARIN   Does she?

MARKUS   Lena, wait outside.

LENA   Know what?

MARKUS   Outside.

LENA   No, tell me what/

KARIN   She doesn't.

LENA   Tell me what you mean!

MARKUS   Go outside!

KARIN   Should I/

LENA   Not until you tell/

KARIN   tell her/

LENA   me what you're/

KARIN   for you?/

LENA   talking about!

KARIN   Are you even capable/

LENA   Stop it/

KARIN   of that?

LENA   Secrets! Always you two, always the two of you…

KARIN   Because I am. Maybe she wants to hear what I have to say.

MARKUS   Outside! Now!

Beat.

LENA   You're out of your mind if you think I'm going to leave
            you alone with her.

MARKUS   *(to KARIN)* Look, what do you want to know?

KARIN   You've been coming in and out of Bonn all this time?

MARKUS   No, I couldn't do that. Lena and I met on… neutral ground.

LENA   Holidays. The Mediterranean. The Riviera. First class,
            not that you'd know anything about that.

MARKUS   Couldn't risk coming to Bonn until recently. *(beat)* Listen,
            I'm sorry that that happened to you. I really am. Is that
            it, are we done here?

KARIN   No, somehow I don't think we're "done here."

LENA   I've had enough of her whining/

KARIN   *(to LENA)* Aren't you even a little bit curious?

LENA   I don't care what you say/

KARIN   A little curious as to why he got involved with you?

LENA   You're jealous.

MARKUS   There's no point/

KARIN   You're scared to know.

LENA   You're delusional.

KARIN   Scared of the answer.

MARKUS   That's enough/

LENA   If it's so damned important/

MARKUS   *(to KARIN)* What do you want?

        KARIN laughs.

KARIN   What do I *want?*

MARKUS   Yes.

KARIN   Haven't you seen enough of my psychological profile to
           know the answer without me telling you? *(beat)* Does
           she know you're Stasi?

LENA   *(relieved)* Of course I do!

KARIN   And you don't care?

LENA   Why should I care? Politics are boring.

KARIN   Maybe because the Stasi have a department dedicated
           to seducing West German women. Maybe because they
           sent Markus to sleep with you.

LENA   What?

MARKUS   That's not/

KARIN   Oh, sorry. "Karl" was sent to sleep with you.

LENA   "Karl"?

KARIN   That's his name.

LENA   You're making this up.

KARIN   I wish I was.

LENA   You're making it up.

KARIN   No, I'm not.

LENA   *(to MARKUS)* Why would you...

KARIN   "Karl Becker" actually.

LENA   ...with me...?

KARIN   What do you have to say, Karl?

    MARKUS stares stonily at KARIN.

LENA   Is that true?

    Beat.

MARKUS   Does it matter?

LENA   Does it matter if you were ordered to sleep with me?

MARKUS   Does it matter if my name is Karl.

LENA   Well, no, but/

MARKUS   I'm the same person.

LENA   But were you/

MARKUS   It doesn't change anything.

LENA   Did they order you to/

MARKUS   This is ridiculous, we need to stop this now/

LENA   sleep with me?

MARKUS   it doesn't matter anymore/

LENA   DID THEY?

         Beat.

MARKUS   No. I was not ordered to sleep with you, Lena.

KARIN   No?

MARKUS   No.

*LENA approaches MARKUS, pauses, and puts her head on
his chest. He pushes her off.*

Stop it.

Beat.

LENA *(quietly)* You chose me. That's what you said. You love me.

KARIN No, that's right, you were just ordered to propose to her.
Maybe you had to after she turned me in.

LENA/MARKUS What?

LENA You were ordered to/

MARKUS What do you mean she turned you in/

LENA propose to me! What the hell/

MARKUS Lena, what did you do?

LENA Do you think you can play me like/

MARKUS Did you/

LENA her? Target me/

MARKUS How could you do that/

LENA I'm not a target, I'm your goddamned equal/

MARKUS   It's despicable and cruel/

LENA   not some mouse on a leash!

MARKUS   and jeopardized the work I was... Lena did you turn her
           in?

LENA   *(mocking)* Markus, were you ordered to propose to me?

MARKUS   Yes.

LENA   Then, yes. Yes I did.

KARIN   You were a target. Same as me.

MARKUS   Not the same/

LENA   No! Not the same! Try! Just try and find someone who's
           as good as me, who make you feel the way I do, who
           keeps your interest, who finds the information you need!
           I dare you! You'll never find anything as sweet as what's
           standing in front you now! THE ENGAGEMENT IS OFF!

           *LENA looks at MARKUS and then runs out of the room,
           slamming the door behind her. Pause.*

KARIN   This is the part where you're supposed to follow her.

MARKUS   She's... volatile.

           Pause.

I should have been there.

KARIN   Yes.

MARKUS   It should have been me.

KARIN   *(quietly)* But it wasn't. Do you care about her?

MARKUS   I guess I do.

KARIN   You guess? Do you love her?

MARKUS   Life isn't as simple as you think it is. *(beat)* I don't know what I'm supposed to say. Listen, Karin, I was encouraged to pursue her interest, I didn't seek her out, they wanted me to work with the situation/

KARIN   You weren't conflicted?

> *MARKUS laughs.*

Why are you laughing?

> *MARKUS shakes his head.*

MARKUS   You have no idea.

KARIN   No, I probably don't. I think I missed a lot of things that should have been obvious.

MARKUS   That was the point, it's designed so that any woman will/

KARIN   Any *woman?*

         MARKUS sighs.

MARKUS   They've tried it with men. It's much less effective.

KARIN   They sent you after/

MARKUS   No! Women, they sent women. The men weren't as… suggestible.

KARIN   Oh, shit!

MARKUS   I don't mean you/

KARIN   Yes. You do! *(beat)* I had nothing to do in jail but think about how I'd been a complete idiot, how I'd been humiliated. But it was tangled up with the crazy desire to just see you again. To have you take it all back, explain it away, and to take me home where we could just finish unpacking the boxes in the living room.

MARKUS   Karin, I'm sorry it turned out this way, if things were different/

KARIN   But that wasn't going to happen. I would lay there wondering if you thought about me at all, or why you went to the trouble to set up a pretend marriage…

MARKUS   You knew?

KARIN   They told me. They told me lots of things.

MARKUS   I did think about you. All the time.

         KARIN laughs.

         I don't expect you to believe me.

         She nods.

         But what you don't understand is that this is all much bigger than you, or me, or Lena, or any of us.

KARIN   Because you were working for the party.

MARKUS   No. Well, yes. This is about creating a better world, a world set up the way it should be.

KARIN   And what kind of world is that?

MARKUS   A world where we're equal, where the minority no longer controls/

KARIN   You did this so that we could all be equal.

MARKUS   Don't be simplistic.

KARIN   No, I'm really trying to understand. I'm trying to understand what was so important that you would go through all of this. That you would put me through all of this. That you would put yourself through all of this.

MARKUS   You're being emotional.

KARIN   And isn't that what attracted you to me? What made it "easier"?

MARKUS   There are personal sacrifices that are sometimes necessary to avoid the exploitation of the masses. I thought you understood this, we talked about it often.

KARIN   It is not the same thing... you... that wasn't what we were discussing. Don't try and make it the same thing. What did you do with the information I gave you?

MARKUS   Passed it along.

KARIN   To the Stasi?

MARKUS   Yes.

KARIN   To who?

MARKUS   My supervisor.

KARIN   Your "father" at our wedding?

MARKUS   This is in the past now, you are obviously able to move on with your life/

KARIN   What did he do with the information?

MARKUS   I don't know. All right, I don't know!

KARIN   I suppose I should be flattered that a whole department
            of the government designed a strategy to produce feel-
            ings of love in me, the mousy secretary.

MARKUS   You shouldn't look at it that way.

KARIN   How should I look at it?

MARKUS   God, Karin, I... okay. I was chosen for you. Just for
            you. They had a profile on you, and they searched for a
            man who looked right, who could act right, who could
            be trained. I was loyal to the party and I fit the bill, so
            I was recruited. For you. They... profiled you... as you
            know, and they coached me on my interactions with
            you. I felt that what I was doing was important, one of
            the most important jobs/

KARIN   A job.

MARKUS   Karin, just listen to me, let me/

KARIN   For months after you disappeared I woke up every day
            not wanting to breathe, not wanting to keep on liv-
            ing, and all you tell me is that there was no magic, just
            mechanics/

MARKUS   Karin, let me finish/

KARIN   Manipulation. The East German government decided to
            make me fall in love. They methodically plotted to make

that come about. Like an assembly line making bicycle parts—put this piece here, put that piece there.

MARKUS   For Chrissake, it wasn't all/

KARIN   A bunch of men sitting around and reading my letters and laughing at me. I DON'T GIVE A SHIT-DAMN ABOUT ESPIONAGE. DID YOU LOVE ME?

           Long pause.

MARKUS   Yes. I loved you. *(beat)* Every time we were apart I'd remember your smile and what it felt like to really laugh with someone. I haven't felt like that in a long time. I'd replay all of the moments we shared together. When I said I couldn't focus because I was thinking about you all the time, I meant it. *(beat)* They pulled me off of your file. Felt I was unstable. I loved you. I wasn't lying about that. I… Is that what you want to hear?

KARIN   That's always been the question, hasn't it? What do *I want to hear?*

MARKUS   What do you want from me?

KARIN   Nothing. I don't want anything from you. They said you'd probably come with her. I didn't really believe them at the time.

MARKUS   What?

KARIN   With Lena. They thought the invitation for coffee would be too delicious for her to pass up, and that she'd throw you into the mix.

MARKUS   Karin, what are you talking about?

KARIN   I'm out for good behaviour. For helping them arrest who they really want. When Hermann Baum died, they saw the opportunity… said if I was "helpful" it could work out well for everyone…

MARKUS   *(getting jumpy)* What the hell are you/

KARIN pulls up the briefcase onto the table.

KARIN   You'll probably recognize this. Variation on a theme. It's been recording our conversation. They probably have her already. They're out front.

MARKUS stands to the side of the window and tries to peer out into the street.

I didn't think she'd actually produce you, but I guess the temptation was too much. Still didn't expect you, when you showed up at the door… I couldn't breathe.

MARKUS quickly looks around the space for alternate exits. He approaches KARIN.

MARKUS   Karin… for what it's worth, there's never been anyone like you. I don't think there ever will be.

Beat.

If things had been different…

KARIN   Then they would have been different.

MARKUS   There's a fire escape through the window in the back.

KARIN   Yes.

MARKUS   You're not going to let me leave that way?

           Very long pause. KARIN makes a decision.

KARIN   No.

           *MARKUS steps back from KARIN, looks out the window,
           then slowly crosses and exits through the door he entered,
           pausing before he closes the door to look at KARIN. He nods.*

           *KARIN picks up the briefcase. Spotlight comes up on KARIN
           standing with the briefcase. She is resolved. Lights fade
           down very slowly.*

           The end.

HISTORICAL NOTES

The Romeo Initiative is loosely based on true events in Cold War Germany. The East German Stasi's "Romeo Initiative" was highly effective, and in place from the 1960s until the fall of the Berlin Wall in 1989. Most of the "relationships" were long-term, from a few years to as many as seventeen or twenty. Some of the women, like Karin, were truly or wilfully blind to what they were involved in. Some others suspected the truth, and others wholeheartedly embraced their role in the espionage.

A few of the female targets were discovered, tried, and jailed for treason. After the fall of the Berlin Wall, the Stasi files were opened up and many more women were tried. Most of the male "Romeos" received amnesty. Most of the women found guilty after the Wall came down were given suspended sentences. Some of them left the country permanently and lived out their lives elsewhere, unable to continue living where these events had transpired.

A CHRONOLOGICAL TIMELINE

Scene Number	Appears in Act	Title
1.	I and II	Black Sea Coast
2.	II	Psych Meeting #1
3.	II	Bookstore
4.	I	The Reception
5.	I	Lunch
6.	II	Markus's Letter
7.	I	Karin's Letter
8.	I and II	A Momentous Date
9.	I	The Panties
10.	II	Psych Meeting #2
11.	II	Documents
12.	II	Psych Meeting #3
13.	II	Lena
14.	I	Jealous
15.	II	Karin's Second Letter
16.	I	Breakup
17.	I	Survival
18.	II	Psych Meeting #4
19.	II	Reconciliation
20.	I	Togetherness
21.	II	Proposal
22.	I and II	Wedding
23.	II	Psych Meeting #5
24.	I and II	An Ending
25.	III	Reunion

ACKNOWLEDGEMENTS

Alberta Theatre Projects, BC Arts Council, Banff Playwrights Colony at the Banff Centre, Canada Council for the Arts, University of Alberta Drama Department, Enbridge playRites Award for Established Artist, La Bella Vita Playwrights Retreat (Vada, Italy), Christian Horn and Marianne Quoirin for German research support, Iris Turcott, Brad Fraser, Clinton Carew, Vern Thiessen, Vicki Stroich, Amy Lynn Strilchuk, Glenda Stirling, Vanessa Porteous, Paul Welch, Heidi Verwey, Shannon Blanchet, Amber Bissonette, Kevin Corey, Kira Bradley, Elena Porter, Celine Stubel, Trevor Leigh, Jamie Konchak, Elinor Holt, Christian Goutsis.

Saskatoon-born Trina Davies is a writer, director, and actor. In 2008 she received the Enbridge playRites Award for Established Artist for *The Romeo Initiative*. Trina has also won awards for *Multi User Dungeon*, *Shatter*, *The Auction*, and *Waxworks*, which have been read and/or performed across Canada. She is currently a member of the Alberta Playwrights Network, the Playwrights Theatre Centre, and the Playwrights Guild of Canada. Trina lives in Vancouver.